MW00477727

Miracles
Still
Happen

Maria Sainz

RED SEAL PUBLISHING

SAN DIEGO, CA

Acknowledgements

"Maria Sainz's book, *Miracles Still Happen*, is a faith lifting, powerful first-hand account of her miraculous healing from cancer. It provides both the drama of the testimony as well as encouragement and practical ways to contend for healing. Maria has taken her testimony, using the power of it to bring faith to others who are struggling with cancer, with miraculous results. I commend this book to you, for your personal edification and a tool to increase other's faith."

Dr. Mike Hutchings,
Director, Global School of Supernatural Ministry and
Global Certification Programs

"Maria's story provides a supernatural testimony of God's love for healing and bringing hope to our world. Maria Sainz is proof that God not only heals and transforms lives, but that He also wants to empower people to walk in His love in such a way that people will know God personally. Maria, and her husband Rick, are special friends who have partnered with me in ministry to further my calling as a pastor and evangelist to serve in the power of the Holy Spirit as we see God transforming lives."

Miles McPherson
Senior Pastor,
The Rock Church, San Diego

"The "dunamis" power (dynamite) found in Acts 1:8 describes the story, testimony and lifestyle of Maria Sainz as a revealed in her new book Miracles still Happen. A must-read for anyone to better understand Holy Spirit's strength, power and ability! Maria is a marvelous example of what Biblical faith, hope, and Holy Spirit love can do with a yielded life."

Larry Peltier M.Div.
Senior Pastor (Ret.)
Encinitas Beach Chapel
Founding Director of Freewater School of Supernatural Discipleship

"Miracles are real; so is God. Jesus saves and heals today. I have seen it happen in America, Brazil, Denmark, Hungary, Canada. In this little book, you will meet a woman for whom it has happened. Maria's story is like thousands I have heard and witnessed in the last few years. It is worth hearing. It is worth believing. It is worth receiving. I met Maria on a Mission to Brazil. She is passionate, wise, kind, and full of the love of God. Open your heart as you open her story. Let the Spirit heal you, move you, pull you deeper into the heart of the Father. His heart is to make you whole."

Dr. Kim Maas
Kim Maas Ministries, Inc.

"Maria Sainz has written a book of hope for anyone facing Cancer. Within these pages you will find encouragement when it is most needed. She speaks from experience giving her earned authority."

Pastors Wayne and Chris Clarke,
His Dwelling Place Ministries

"Maria's healing from breast cancer is a testament that God still heals today. While not discounting the path to pursue a medical intervention, she pushed into what only God could do. Her story is like many who are looking for God to intervene with a miracle and her healing gives hope to those who may have lost all hope. Be encouraged as you read her testimony."

Dr. Rodney Hogue

"I was diagnosed with cancer in 2002. My daughter-in-law on hearing the report felt in her spirit that this would not take my life. That was fifteen years ago and I have been cancer free ever since. The Bible says, for the testimony of Jesus (the things He did and continues to do, healing, miracles, etc.) is the spirit of prophecy. In other words Maria's testimony and mine of supernatural healing of cancer, not once but twice in her life, is a declaration that He can and will heal you of cancer, or whatever disease has been your diagnosis. From Genesis through the whole of the Bible God healed and He has never stopped healing. He will use your faith, the amount of faith you have right now no matter how small. Faith and Hope... step out and receive your miracle. Take hold of God's goodness and our testimonies of Jesus as yours, today."

Joe Vaine, Missionary Pilot
Flying For Jesus

"The healing power of heaven is released through Maria's miraculous testimony of victory over breast cancer! She is on the offensive, boldly taking on cancer in the authority of Christ. Her story will compel and inspire you to discover and lean into the goodness of God, and His perfect love in the midst of adversity. If you are dealing with illness and you are in need of hope in this season, let your faith for healing arise as you read this book. The time is now for the collective faith of the body of Christ to ignite the eradication of all illness, because Jesus paid for all that and more!"

Bourne Burns
Senior Pastor,
Beach Chapel

"The Scripture indicates that we all have a measurable source of faith, (measure) Romans 12:3 beginning with saving faith, and episodes of supernatural faith (1 Corinthians 11:9). But when you have had a personal encounter with faith like Maria, an encounter in which God releases a miraculous infusion of faith that set her free from cancer, you come out of that experience with a stubborn faith. This is how Maria now lives, and what this book is all about. Get ready for a new ride of faith, with a God who still does miracles."

Gary Goodell
Third Day Churches, Inc.
Author of *Permission Has Been Granted To Do Church Differently in the 21st Century* and *Where Would Jesus Lead*

I dedicate this book to John and Michelle Boyd and their two children, Sarah and Noah! These friends have been there for Rick and I through the roughest of trials and the greatest of triumphs. Never once did they lose hope on us but supported our every endeavor when we stepped out into unknown waters. Their unending support, prayer and encouragement held us up. They believed in us when some didn't. We are blessed beyond words for our friendship.

Contents

Foreword

Walking through cancer with your loved one is brutal. Living through the range of emotions that are attached to the word "cancer" is unthinkable. Watching the mental and physical battle attack on Maria tried to render me helpless, but I knew I had to stand strong against this menacing disease. It tries to break your will to submit to its power, but I could not let that happen. As Maria mustered her strength to fight, I had to as well.

Writing a forward for my wife's book is an honor and an incredible blessing just as she is. She is a rock solid believer in the Word of God, and knows how it really works to properly apply it to your life. Maria took the core principals of healing and applied them to herself and said, "God we are going to do this your way"!

You may have cancer now or know someone that does. I watched first-hand how Maria put herself fully into the hands of God! I'm not here to tell you it was easy but to encourage you that "Miracles Still Happen".

Rick Sainz

Preface

For every person who has encountered the excruciatingly horrid diagnosis of cancer, may this testimony inspire you to believe beyond the assault...for a miracle!

This is a candid look at my personal story and the process of being healed from breast cancer. It is a culmination of a five-month process that came to a finish in Sao Paulo, Brazil on a mission's trip with Global Awakening.

Battles are pruning seasons. Yet, really, they are more like opportunities for God to move miraculously into these so-called impossible situations.

Once I got past the initial blow of the diagnosis of cancer, and after a ridiculous amount of sobbing, I moved forward pressing into God. With everything in me, I sought after the prize of being close to Him more than anything else. In that place of confident rest, the brutal trial of impossibilities suddenly became a breeding ground for the possible. Faith pleases God because it reveals our hearts to trust Him.

I've seen God do many amazing things in my life, which I will share later in this story.

I'm sure if you thought about it, you'd be reminded of all the wonderful things God has done to save, heal, and deliver you.

Faith requires RISK. We must believe beyond what we see in the natural and stand on the Promises of God. These are available now through Jesus' death on the cross.

Only as we move past the attacks of the enemy who attempts to steal our joy, peace and strength, do we allow God to do what He delights in doing for those He loves. And it's in these moments that the revelation of God's goodness penetrates our hearts.

In the midst of our battles, Jesus cleverly reveals himself, beautifully, giving us our story, and showing his mighty hand upon the situation. Jesus magnificently weaves Himself into the fabric of our lives. Our stories become this grandiose tapestry intertwined into each other's lives. These stories become our inheritance and catalysts to more testimonies.

The power of God is still alive today! The power of the testimony opens up the realm for more opportunities for God to do it again.

Miracles still do happen!

Do it again, Lord! All to your Glory!

Introduction

In June of 2015, the week after my husband, Rick, and I were ordained as pastors in our nonprofit organization called Red Seal ministries, I was diagnosed with breast cancer. Prior to this I'd undergone several routine mammograms and ultrasounds, but since our shift into full-time ministry, and big changes in our medical insurance, I hadn't had a mammogram in almost three years. Wondering if this was the reason for such scrutiny, I agreed to the two biopsies in both breasts, because they showed several questionable clusters of cells and calcifications. After a month of recovery, I was called into the medical office to review the test results.

When we met with the nurse practitioner to go over the results, I sensed something was about to happen that I could not be prepared for.

We sat in a cold austere room for about fifteen minutes before she briskly entered the room and shut the door. Somehow, her friendly smile and kind demeanor didn't comfort me.

As we made small talk, she glanced at the reports. Putting the papers on her lap she looked sternly at Rick, and me.

She mustered the words and abruptly said,

"It's cancer."

"What?" I responded.

I stared intently as she looked down at the papers and fidgeted. Then, she lifted her head and looked directly at me.

"Yes, it's cancer," she said firmly.

"It's called incito carcinoma. The cells are contained in a sac within the duct," she continued.

Shocked and in denial, I spit out the words, "I don't have cancer."

No matter how many times she attempted to ease the blow from the news, I couldn't be relieved. Excruciating pressure erupted in my gut. I couldn't stand being in that room a minute longer. To add fuel to the fire, she regurgitated a bunch of spiritual verbiage I didn't identify with. We complied with her directive and agreed to meet with an oncologist right away.

We abruptly got up and bolted out the door, and I exploded into hysterical sobbing. Tears flooded down my face. Barely able to see, I stumbled to our car. Rick calmly drove, "It's going to be okay," he said.

Attempting to soothe my pain, he reached across and placed his hand on my lap. We'd already walked through many torrential storms and I encouraged myself that we'd get through this, too.

CHAPTER 1

The Assault

I WILL SAY TO GOD MY ROCK,
"WHY HAVE YOU FORGOTTEN ME?
WHY DO I GO MOURNING BECAUSE OF
THE OPPRESSION OF THE ENEMY?"

PSALM 42:9

WE ARRIVED HOME FROM the doctor's office after that grue-some diagnosis, I scurried to the bedroom, closed the door be-hind me, and slipped into a dark cocoon.

Is this really happening? I'm in the healing ministry!

Fear and anger consumed my thoughts.

I had been through so much tribulation this year. I thought what I had endured was now over. And then this!

I sat on my bed and wiped my raw swollen eyes. With every-thing in me, I screamed to God,

"What do you have to say about Cancer? I'm going to do this your way."

I waited. I cried out again,

"What do YOU have to say about Cancer?"

Narrowing my gaze onto the Bible that was right in front of me on the bed, I leaned forward, to place my hand on the tattered red leather cover. Then, I boldly asked,

"Lord, give me a scripture? I need to hear from you right now!"

Stalling, my fingers released, and I flung open the Bible. My eyes zoomed in on 2 Timothy 2:17. Shocked at what I saw, I read it out loud,

"...And their message will spread like cancer. Hymenaeus and Philetus are of this sort,"

What? The word cancer is in the Bible?

I took a closer look for context, and read the previous verses.

2 Timothy 2:15-19 (NKJV)

15 Be diligent to present yourself approved to God, a worker who does not need to be ashamed, rightly dividing the word of Truth.

16 But shun profane and idle babblings, for they will increase to more ungodliness.

17 And their message will spread like cancer. Hymenaeus and Philetus are of this sort,

18 who have strayed concerning the truth, saying that the resurrection is already past; and they overthrow the faith of some.

19 Nevertheless the solid foundation of God stands, having this seal: "The Lord knows those who are His," and, "let everyone who names the name of Christ depart from iniquity."

After further investigation, I found that "cancer" is only one time in the entire Bible.

God knew how to get my attention. I paused and meditated on these Scriptures, and I asked the Holy Spirit to penetrate my heart with His Truth as I waited.

"I'm open to hear you, Father. I want your Truth more than anything else."

These two men, Hymenaeus and Philetus had moved away from the Truth. They were influencing those around them with a wrong message. What they said had enough impact that it traveled as fast as cancer.

IS THERE A CONNECTION BETWEEN CANCER AND OUR WORDS?

We all have cancer cells in our bodies and, if left undetected over a period of time, these cells can get out of control. Cancer is known to spread fast once it gets to that point. The toxic cancer cells cluster and can turn into large tumors in many instances.

Let's read more...

In verse 16 the word idle in the Greek is argos, and it means worthless and barren words. Dead works. Lazy, shunning the labor which one ought to perform!

MATTHEW 12:36 SAYS,

"But I say to you that for every idle word men may speak, they will give account of it in the Day of Judgment."

In this context, the word "Idle" here means, "ineffective, and a word unaccompanied by works." Dead works are anything that has no effect for life or God's kingdom. Dead works have no good power to move on God's behalf.

Our words have more impact than we realize. Our words carry weight. They're containers of power. Whatever the words, they affect the atmosphere around us. Negative words wreak havoc on our life causing a negative impact. If we stay focused on what the enemy is doing, before we know it our words will match what we are experiencing. Eventually, we breed an atmosphere for a curse. It was a sobering reality to see this. Have you ever noticed how it feels like a bullet between the eyes, when God shows you some area in your life that's a blind spot? But when you get the revelation God wants for you to know and experience, it's...FREEDOM!

This is what God is saying here. He's warning us to not fall prey to a tactic of the enemy in our lives. Otherwise, if we don't deal with the issues of life as they come up, we will end up carrying around a Poop backpack. No one sees what's in it by looking at the outside; but after a while a rancid stench will erupt. If it's not dealt with the smell becomes so familiar you can't detect it any longer.

God had been speaking to me about my reactions to a stressful season, but I didn't really come to a full understanding of what I was holding onto so tightly until the diagnosis.

Awestruck by God's invitation, this supernatural sign opened my heart to be more vulnerable with Him. It's His kindness that leads us to repentance.

After a year and a half of intensely difficult times dealing with family, ministry and relationships, I buckled under the pressure. Most of those months felt like a fire hose barreling down me 24/7. I thought I was holding it all together. I prayed, studied, and did all the things I knew to do when under pressure.

Prophetic words brought encouragement to us in rough seasons, to stay on track and not give up.

Earlier that year in March of 2014, Rick and I visited a bible study at Blaine Cook's home in Southern California. We were seated across from a man who looked familiar. He was bald, carried a distinctly strong presence of God, and oozed incredible love and joy. I couldn't recall why this man looked so familiar. Soon it came it came to me. I discreetly elbowed Rick in his side and whispered,

"That guy was in "Father of Lights" movie. His name is Robby Dawkins."

Rick nodded as the meeting got underway. Robby began prophesying words of encouragement over many people in the room. Then, Rick was highlighted to Robby. He gave a word to Rick and said, "You're going to be the one writing the checks for the revival in San Diego."

Then, He looked over at me and said to Rick, "Is she with you?"

"Yes." Rick replied.

He looked at me and said, "You are under intense warfare. It's a family member. It will lift within 6 months."

Nice! Really God? Six months?

Instead of being grateful, I cringed. Once I got over myself, I realized the word gave me an ending point for the craziness I was experiencing. I was relieved it was not all in my mind. Sometimes, when you feel like you are in a pressure cooker, no matter how obedient you try to be, it still doesn't seem like you're doing what is right in the sight of God. Often times I've beat myself up as I attempted to juggle all the responsibilities in front of me.

The prophetic word Robby gave me was fulfilled, and all the chaos lifted exactly six months later. This really strengthened my faith knowing there was an end date to the mayhem.

What do you do when the pressure gets too hard? I don't know about you, but I don't like being put to any test. I like the challenge at first, but I'll feel like a failure after it's gone on too long, wondering what I did to cause it.

Disciplining from God can be hard, but necessary, to go higher. What the enemy uses to take us out, God uses to give us greater understanding of His love and Truth. He's calling us to reach for higher levels of greatness.

Intimacy is the key that brings greater awareness of His presence. In His presence, the answers are found. It's in that place where revelation becomes more apparent. Solutions and strategies are revealed to help us move forward. A deeper intimacy with God brings the direction we need to move forward and trust for breakthrough.

There are no shortcuts in the kingdom of God. As much as we'd like to, we can't skip the hard stuff. Pruning hurts for a season and then we're better for it.

God loves us so much he clips us. Have you ever seen how a grapevine looks when it's been pruned back? It looks dead! That's exactly how we need to be. We must cut back those things that hinder a kingdom lifestyle.

In the gospel of John chapter 15 it explains how being dead to a self-centered lifestyle is a key mindset for the pruning. Anything that doesn't draw us to God, becomes a hindrance toward our destiny. When we abide in Him, we'll bear much fruit in our lives. He is the vine and we are the branches. Without His constant input and guidance through the Holy Spirit, we will not bear fruit. We will become stagnant in old thinking and old ways.

In this process of healing, I came to a clear realization I might as well get used to seasons of cuts and blows. Ultimately, I'm after the transformation.

Keeping an open dialogue with the Holy Spirit enabled me to make sense of the trial. You can always bank on God having your best interests at heart. Keeping an open honest dialogue with God keeps us pruned.

If we lose our lives for His namesake, we will gain them back in greater measure. We'll come out better in the end and that's what gives more weight to influence those around you and bring greater Glory to God.

CHAPTER 2

Our Words Matter

DEATH AND LIFE ARE IN THE POWER OF THE TONGUE,
AND THOSE WHO LOVE IT WILL EAT ITS FRUIT.

PROVERBS 18:2

SO, WHAT'S GOD PRUNING? Perhaps, we can start with our attitudes, mindsets, and words.

Wouldn't hurt if we did a negativity fast?

Well, that's exactly what I did. I began taking inventory of everything spewing out of my mouth.

In January of 2015 I had a dream. In the dream God showed me how my words were affecting my life.

In this dream, I was taken into an elevator going down representing (lower level) living and into an underground cave. When the doors opened I walked into a cosmetics department. I looked around and saw a woman at the counter in a wheelchair. I started helping her find a lipstick. In that moment, I became the sales clerk and found her a red lipstick that she liked and I sold it to her. When I was done I went back into the elevator. It took me up (higher levels of living) and when the doors opened, I was now in a place that appeared to be a huge beautiful resort.

That morning after the dream, I had a friend interpret the dream and he gave me some insights to the details. I will only highlight a few things. Basically, this lower level cave represented a stronghold. I was helping a woman find a lipstick in a cosmetics department, representing the vanity of the woman in a wheelchair who much greater needs. The lipstick represented my words and red signified sinful words!

I have a stronghold with my words? God, reveal what words are not pleasing to you? I don't understand.

Often times our blind spots are mindsets that we have had for years. Words are such deeply ingrained strongholds. They are not easily detected, and can only be enlightened through the Holy Spirit.

That morning, as I walked on a street I've walked for years with my Golden Retriever Savannah, I talked to the Lord about this dream. I asked and listened over and over. Nonchalantly, I turned and shifted my gaze to a car license plate that read,

"Talk right"

By now, I shouldn't be startled by God's surprises. He shows up just at the right time. His voice speaks Truth into any lie of the enemy.

"What? You want me to clean up how I talk?"

Over the next several months, I became acutely aware of everything I was saying. I continued to seek God as best I knew how. Our negative words can create an atmosphere for a curse.

WHAT DO YOUR WORDS SOUND LIKE?

If your words sound kind, loving, and laced with grace the Father is pleased.

Are your words graced with love? Are your words slicing and dicing others? Including you?

James 1:26-27 says, "If anyone among you thinks he is religious, and does not bridle his tongue but deceives his own heart, this one's religion is useless."

Our ability to speak was given to us to bless. We were created in His image. (Genesis 3) God spoke the world into existence and the universe is held together by His very Words.

John 1:1 says, "In the beginning was the Word, and the Word was with God, and the Word was God."

Everything God says is unmovable without His consent. He is the Word. His Words are who He is and embody His nature. His Word makes us alive. He is the bread of life. His Word is a promise and He is not one to lie. His promises are activated through faith. If we believe His word, His nature now comes alive in us! When we speak His Word and who He is through us outwardly, it brings life to others.

If we are made in God's image, we have been given the same power to advance His kingdom on earth. He created us to look and act like God. He's empowered us through the Holy Spirit to be like Him. If God speaks and things change, then when we speak we have that same potential to shift things like God does.

Take for instance the weather patterns. I watched a You Tubes video of a man who spoke to a tornado and commanded it to move and go the other direction when people were threatened. Soon after He said it, the tornado shifted direction and went away. Those people threatened were now safe.

We have that much power? Yes, because God intended for us to bring His Kingdom on earth. In other words, we get to be God's representatives. With that mandate He gave us His, authority over the enemy and over any circumstance.

Do you believe you have authority over the enemy?

The problem arises when we try to activate it and we don't see it work. We must persevere in our growing process and keep learning.

Stretch your faith to take the risks necessary to see it happen. When our faith propels those words spoken out into a dark atmosphere it releases light. Think about what you say to people. Are you words uplifting or critical? What we say either attracts heaven or hell. When we complain, murmur, and backbite, hell is attracted to us.

My friend, Rodney Hogue puts it this way, "Complaining is the worship of hell, and praising is the worship of Heaven."

When we praise God by saying positive things about our life and others, Heaven is attracted to us.

WHAT DO YOU WANT ATTRACTED TO YOU?

Our words are generally connected to our attitudes and mindsets.

Proverbs 23:7 says, "As a man thinks in his heart, so is he."

What we believe is what will come out of our mouth. You may be surprised by some of the things you say. Have you ever considered that some words may not seem like they match your heart, but they still come out? That might be an indication to do some soul surgery.

You may be asking yourself right now,

"Why do I say those things? I don't like the negative things I say."

We must have a perspective of pursuing change and these moments offer us an opportunity for an upgrade.

We have the power to overcome circumstances around us and change the way we think and the words we say.

WE'RE MORE POWERFUL THAN WE REALIZE.

God gave us power. However, when we align with the accuser and speak negatively into our situations or life, we breed an atmosphere of negativity. Then, negative things will happen. Complaining has that same effect. The word, "complain", means to remain. When we gripe, does it remain with us? Have you ever noticed that when you talk about a negative situation, you can feel the atmosphere of those words? If we get worked up enough we're not only affected but so is the person we are sharing with.

If we stay fixed on Him, we can keep ourselves thinking on things that are lovely, true and of good report. (Phil 3:14) What we say is what's in our hearts.

Out of the mouth proceeds what's in the heart of a man.

Look at Matthew 15:18, "But those things which proceed out of the mouth come from the heart, and they defile a man."

WHAT'S IN YOUR HEART?

I know for myself, if I don't go after God, pursuing to know Him more, I've missed the meaning of my entire existence. What do you think pleases our Heavenly Father? After all, He's done it all for us. If our hearts are after God's heart, we'll choose to live a righteous life, and it will keep us from discontentment, and disappointment. I believe that with this focus in mind our words change.

My husband, Rick, had a friend who would often say, "I open my mouth and stuff falls out."

I don't know about you, but that's not something I want to be known for!

What we speak opens the door for the enemy or for Heaven. If we speak negativity, we align with the enemy and open ourselves up to the fruit of it. What we say we get to eat the fruit of it. We will reap what we sow.

Often, when we are going through the fire and the battle gets too hot, we tend to veer off course for a season. It's a time to connect with God at a deeper level, right? We do most of our growing in the trials. Look for the treasure in every trial. It's strengthening to look where God is working. When we speak faith-filled words it goes into the spiritual realm and pulls out what is there.

On the other hand, if we complain it brings with it a critical spirit.

Look at what Matthew 7:3 says, "And why do you look at the speck in your brother's eye, but do not consider the plank in your own eye?"

If we are focused on all the bad things that people are doing wrong, we've become judges and then we bring an attack on ourselves. If we also focus on all the horrible things going on in the world, eventually we will get depressed.

Why? Because that's what our minds are fixed on. When we give God opportunity to move, and we declare with our faith-filled positive words, faith shifts the atmosphere and that's what breeds a miracle.

Our words demand to be fulfilled and call forth what we say with power. This brings miracles into existence.

That make us incredibly powerful people wouldn't you say? It's in our confessing and declaring that brings the Word into reality. Our words can bring positive or negative results. We can tear down, or build up.

Ephesians 4:29, "Let no corrupt word proceed out of your mouth but what is good and necessary edification that it may impart grace to the hearers."

Grace is the empowerment to do God's will. We have the privilege of continuing to impart grace to others through our words.

We often we don't hear our own words. We must continually impart grace to ourselves through our words and receive the grace of God toward ourselves.

What we believe is most often what we say. If we change our beliefs, we change our words.

One way to start making strides to move forward, even if our circumstances haven't changed, is calling it forth with our words until it manifests. Say it until you believe it.

Romans 4:17 says, "Calling forth what isn't as if it were."

Our words have so much power they are honored by God or the enemy. The two kingdoms oppose each other. It can also be visible through what we say. Who we align with is what we represent in that moment. It is indicative of our words.

God made us in His image to say things that will bring about a reality of His goodness and love wherever we go and whatever we do. Ultimately, in this current spiritual war, it takes a continual choice to not agree with the devil because one of his tactics is to get us off-kilter. When he succeeds we speak negativity.

Through my process I chose by my faith, to keep focused on God's Truth. I chose to deny any feelings that brought doubt and unbelief. The more I stayed fixed on Jesus the more peace came to me. (Isaiah 26:3)

What we say has so much weight that God gave us the ability to create whatever atmosphere we want. One of the main pathways is through our words.

There are spiritual laws in place on earth right now. What we talk about will be attracted toward us.

The law of lift is the force of energy that science shows causes the plane to take flight.

Then there is the law of gravity; if you throw something up in the air it immediately comes down; it doesn't stay suspended in mid-air, but it falls right down.

The law of attraction is the attractive, magnetic power of the Universe that draws similar energies together. It manifests through creation, everywhere and in many ways. Even the law of gravity is part of the law of attraction. This law attracts thoughts, ideas, people, situations and circumstances.

These laws are in place regardless if we are with God or not. These laws can work for you or against you based on how each law works.

Also, the law of attraction is connected to our words and thoughts. What we say can affect our life. If we continually say negative, doubtful, hateful, discouraging words, we will eat of the fruit of those words and guess what? What we've been saying for months and years becomes our reality. I often hear people blaming God for the cancer, or sickness or bad things happening in their lives. Like we are supposed to live this passive life where God is supposed to just bail us out without any relationship or connection to Him at all. God is not magic genie. God is a person and He is not required to just do what we want. Rather, when we seek him with a holy pursuit to know Him deeply, we discover how good He really is, and in that place of intimacy, our actions and words will align with His heart.

If you say words that criticize and hurt people you will attract a curse or the negative effects of those words to your life! That's powerful Truth right there.

We can live a lifestyle of appropriating this law into our lives. God has given us a powerful tool to overcome the enemy's tactics to steal our joy, peace and health. God desires to bless us and it's His will for us to experience a prosperous and abundant life. (John 10:10)

We can say what God would say and we can do His will.

If we belong to God, then Jesus has given us authority to use our words to accomplish great and mighty things to advance His kingdom on earth. Our words are containers of power.

HOW DO YOU WANT TO USE YOUR POWER?

Align with God's promises and declare that for your life the blessings. The promises He's laid out before you are an inheritance belonging to Him. Don't align with any negative thing said about you from the past.

During this time, I became acutely aware of any attitudes contrary to God's love and Truth. When I got negative, I would go away and worship. Often times after doctors appointments I'd get discouraged and assaulted with fear and it would creep in to derail my faith.

Instead, I declared God's word over myself and spoke things like,

""No cancer cells can live in my body"

"By His stripes I am healed. You sent your word and healed me."

"I am healed in Jesus name."

"Tumors are of the past and no tumor can live in my body."

Proverbs 12:25 says, "Anxiety in the heart of a man causes depression, but a good word makes it glad."

Its amazing revelation when we truly understand the power of a good word over ourselves to change our emotions from worry to gladness.

Philippians 4:6, tells us to be thankful and then we can change our surroundings and establish a life protected by peace.

I discovered after I made these bold declarations I would feel better.

Sometimes the best medicine is saying something different. Weigh your words. Then declare the opposite of the negative thing that is happening in the natural. Even though it's a natural fact, it doesn't mean it has to stay that way. The more we focus on the negativity of a situation the worse the circumstances become. Our minds run wild and we will find a million reasons why things will go wrong; then they do.

Instead, if you want to be on your way to a free, and joyful lifestyle, recalibrate your focus onto the promises of God. When we do, eventually our faith is stirred to believe. Before you know it, the outcome is good; and it's way better than before.

God's Word is life. His Word is sharper than a two-edged sword. Perhaps, we can apply the Word to our hearts to do the surgery needed for our soul.

One of our weapons to overcoming the enemy is living in a place of joy.

I remember waiting for my healing and doing all I knew to stand on God's Word. But the waiting brought me fatigue, discouragement, and depression.

I decided to speak out words that were what I wanted. I said things like,

"I am filled with the abundant joy of the Lord. In your presence is fullness of joy. You restored the joy of my salvation. I am walking in supernatural health. I am healed."

I kept declaring these statements and many more over myself. Actually, I made a decision to speak about 100 declarations a day even if I didn't fully believe them all. As I spoke these words out loud, my body didn't necessary stand there scrutinizing or analyzing my words. My brain doesn't know the difference what words I say either. But my body and anything surrounding me will respond to my words.

After a few days of speaking these statements I started to feel better. I remember feeling in a really good mood and wondering why.

I asked God, "Why am I in such a good mood?"

I saw this picture of God as a Father with white fluffy hair and this huge smile on His face responding to me,

"I'm always in a good mood. You're only reflecting the nature of your Daddy!"

When we speak godly, loving, and faith-filled words, we show love to those around us and ourselves. We are agreeing with what our Heavenly Father had in mind when He made us.

When we speak, light is emitted. It's been scientifically proven that our words affect our bodies at the cellular level.

Every cell in the body emits more than 100,000 light impulses or photons per second. These light emissions, are called biophotons, and have been found to be the steering mechanism behind all biochemical reactions.

The body uses biophotons as information packages to send signals from one point to another in much the same way that fiber-optic cables transmit signals using light. Biophotons carry information about the state of the body; because healthy cells, sick cells, tumor cells, infectious viruses and bacteria have different light signals. Biophotons, like all photons, can form either a pattern of coherence, where individual light frequencies complement each other as in laser light, or chaos, where individual frequencies are disordered.

Our words change and affect the well being of our bodies. These biophotons reveal the science behind how we are affected by words.

Isn't it time we start speaking like God and the manner in which He designed us?

We are powerful to bring healing to ourselves and to others through what we choose to say.

I continued seeking God to find any area in my heart that wasn't' right with Him. Then, and only then, could I start to recognize the blind areas where I was cursing myself.

Once we allow God to do the surgery on our hearts , and we've humbly dealt with our own stuff, we come out the other side with miraculous transformation. This change is revealed through our words and attitudes.

Then through His grace, He uses us to reveal breakthrough to others, and we have the privilege of bringing restoration to them.

CHAPTER 3

Forgiveness

FOR IF YOU FORGIVE MEN THEIR TRESPASSES, YOUR
HEAVENLY FATHER WILL ALSO FORGIVE YOU.

MATTHEW 6:14

IMMEDIATELY AFTER I GOT the news of the diagnosis, I contacted two powerful women pastors, Audrey and Chris, who quickly cleared their schedules to meet with me for personal ministry. I meant business and I needed some help to go after God. Their help would enable me to find my blind spots.

Several days later, I met with them at their office. In our four-hour long ministry time, they went after any root issues. They attentively listened.

I admire them for all they have overcome in their lives. Through their love and wisdom, I knew I'd get more answers to this cancer issue.

They assessed some of the core beliefs that were triggers to causing some of my disappointments. These underlying unresolved disappointments were at the core of some blockages.

As they spoke the Truth with love, I was able to be vulnerable and cooperative with the Holy Spirit.

Audrey, candidly shared her own personal experience with breast cancer which occurred before she gave her life to Jesus. Tenderly and simple, she coached me on what to expect with doctors, appointments and all the many complexities involving all the procedures.

God confirmed what gnawed at the root of my turmoil. Much of what was unpacked was unresolved unforgiveness from some past traumas.

I thought I had dealt with these years ago? I teach this.

We don't arrive. Our relationship with God is an ongoing process. Life is often times a continual transitioning into the next level of revelation. We achieve progressively better understanding of who we are and who God is. Our true identity is revealed as we mature. As we walk through the trials of our lives and choose to allow God to mold us into His image, we are being changed from glory to glory.

When we forgive, within the process of life, we stay clear of letting anything get in the way of our destiny and purpose for our lives. Forgiveness is the single most amazing promise and blessing Jesus gave us to live the abundant life!

2014 through 2016 were rough years spent sorting out the process of becoming my mother's power of attorney, and making decisions on her behalf. After a grueling process of getting her diagnosed with intermediate stages of dementia, there were many steps to place her in a home. Although, God never once left me hanging and He supplied all the resources to get her into the perfect place, it was extremely stressful, as those that have stepped into the role of caregiver know.

I'd been a full-time caregiver to my mother-in-law from 2000-2003. It was an incredible time filled with restoration, and a multitude of miracles for my husband's family. During this time, we saw God heal my mother-in-law in so many ways. At eighty-five years old, she was set free of years of bondage, and got a second lease on life, finding a deep intimacy with Jesus. The silver lining, in this difficult task, was seeing her fall madly in love with Jesus. It's never too late to find your identity. She not only found it, but she gave that away as a legacy to her family after she passed on to be with the Lord on November 2003.

The situation with my mom seemed more difficult. It was emotionally challenging with all I had to do: sell her belongings, liquidate her properties, and make believe to my mom all was normal. Simultaneously, doing full time ministry made things exponentially harder. After a while, the responsibilities of running our ministry began to wear me down.

Later, I discovered the enemy uses these things to get us tired. When we are tired our guard is down, we are vulnerable and weaker. In our weaknesses he attacks the hardest.

Thank God for His grace to do what He's called us to do.

In the midst of a battle you can't explain in the moment, we can stand on God's Truth to see to it His promises will manifest, even in the waiting. So many things happened all at once, that made the attack overwhelming.

Around this time, I took Rick to the ER and found blood clots in his lungs and in his right leg. The doctor immediately admitted him into ICU. Even though Rick was quite coherent looked healthy, according to the doctors, his life was tremendously threatened beyond could comprehend.

The next day, I received a phone call that my mother was in Palomar Hospital's ER! I abruptly left the hospital with Rick, to go to the other side of the city to be with of my mother.

For several weeks of driving back and forth between two hospitals! Both my husband and my mother escaped death that week!

Around the same time, we were being attacked in the ministry and I really never thought I'd experience that kind of persecution in our country. We felt overwhelmed by what took place. I won't go into all the details for this book, but God strengthened us and gave us a Heavenly perspective that sustained us to stay grounded in love. Although, persecution in other countries certainly far outweighs what we experienced it didn't minimize the excruciating pressure we felt.

James 5:16 says, "Confess your trespasses to one another, and pray for one another, that you may be healed. The effective, fervent prayer of a righteous man avails much."

Unforgiveness is totally contrary to who God is and how He thinks, speaks, and acts. Therefore, He cannot bless us when we are in agreement with that fallen kingdom. Spirits of bitterness will tempt us to agree with it, and before we know it we are being tormented.

When we keep a record of wrong against another, we are saying that they owe us a debt on the accounting books of our heart. This is not good for us or the other person. When we hold a debt, we actually attach all of their stuff to us.

When we forgive, we unload that "poop" backpack and in its place get a shiny one filled with peace and joy, with the aroma of Heaven.

Mark 11:25-26 says, "And when ye stand praying, forgive, if you have ought against any: that your Father also which is in heaven may forgive you your trespasses. But if you do not forgive, neither will your Father which is in heaven forgive your trespasses."

HOW IS YOUR ACCOUNT TOWARD OTHERS IN YOUR HEART? WHAT ABOUT YOURSELF?

When the Father sent His Son Jesus Christ of Nazareth to die for the sins of the world, He gave us the ability to be forgiven of our debts and for us to forgive others of their debts toward us. We've been empowered to be victorious. The key is if we will choose to let go of our rights and allow Jesus to judge the offender on our behalf. That's the kind of Heavenly Father we have. His justice is righteous and He is faithful. He redeems what the enemy has done to us through others and makes it right.

In my personal ministry time, the two amazing women warriors enabled me to deal with the trauma of the last couple of years and some personal disappointments. Sometimes we don't realize that we tolerate and harbor disappointments of the past things that didn't turn out the way we expected.

I always thought I'd have children. I remember having conversations right after getting married about a family. We had no idea that after three years of being married, we'd become full time caregivers to Rick's mother.

The first year while caring for his mother, I miscarried. It was rougher for Rick than me, although extremely sorrowful for me too. We moved past it; we continued to care for Rick's mother for about three years. Later, after her passing, we still never had children. It seemed like we'd make it happen, but things never did; My husband now admits that his passivity, was due to the fear of me miscarrying again, just like his mother did when he was three years old. He lost a baby brother. He and his mother went through a rough time of grieving because Rick's dad didn't allow them to cry or show any kind of emotion. All this came out when Rick went for his personal ministry with our pastors as well during this process. Rick went for these long ministry sessions initially because he wanted to do whatever he could to move us forward in our marriage, our ministry and of course, my healing. Actually, these ministry sessions proved to be beneficial for Rick as it uncovered some of the roots to his issues. I appreciated him that he'd do whatever was needed to bring us into a healthier place in our relationship. I had heard stories where spouses leave when one is diagnosed with cancer!

I was grateful to discovery of one of my own personal blind spots; after years of thinking I was okay with the idea of never having kids, that I actually never got over it. In the ministry time, I allowed God into those hidden crevices of my heart, forgave. Almost immediately, I experienced a lightness and anticipation with God I hadn't felt in a long time!

I don't know about you, but when we agree with the enemy and his ways, we feel tormented. Whether it's fear or anger, it feels like you're all knotted up inside. That day I felt unraveled and free.

Do you recall the story in Matthew 18 when Jesus challenges us about the debts? The master forgives the servant of an exorbitant debt,(in our day about a million dollars), but then the servant attacks another person who owes him a measly hundred dollars or so, because he was unwilling to forgive the small debt.

Here's what Matthew 18:34-35 says, "And his master was angry, and delivered him to the torturers until he should pay all that was due to him. So My heavenly Father also will do to you if each of you, from his heart, does not forgive his brother his trespasses."

That's sobering, but freeing, to see this from our Heavenly Father's perspective.

God wants us healthy, free, and joyful.

He never designed us to carry this kind of weight or torment. Eventually, it will take a toll on us physically.

I was free from that stronghold that day. I carried on with a newfound perspective, knowing through the power of the Holy Spirit, I am able to live an unoffended life all of my days. You can too.

God is saying to you today, "When you go through deep waters, I will be with you. When you go through rivers of difficulty, you will not drown. When you walk through the fire of oppression, you will not be burned up. You are Mine." (Isaiah 43:2)

CHAPTER 4

Stones of Remembrance

MARVELOUS THINGS HE DID
IN THE SIGHT OF THEIR FATHERS,
IN THE LAND OF EGYPT, IN THE FIELD OF ZOAN.

PSALM 78:12

ONE OF OUR WEAPONS of warfare in a battle is to remember His goodness and all He's done in the past. When we recall the good things, it stirs up faith to stand on the promises of God.

On my initial office visit with the oncologist, I listened to the grueling details of what He was about to do to me. Overwhelmed, I tried to hide my emotions from Rick. He'd get upset when I got tense or stressed.

Motionless, I sat in my passenger seat next to him. Tears streamed down my face.

"Do you want to go to Staples?" He asked.

Like I care to go shopping right now.

"No, I'll wait here." I retorted.

"I need to go to Staples to get something." He added.

No response. Ignoring his request I turned away looking out the window.

"C'mon? I need to get something and I want you to come."

"Alright, fine." I grunted.

Angrily, I grabbed my purse and got out of the car. Rick went in a different direction to find what he came there for, and I wandered aimlessly up and down the isles. Slowly dragging my feet, my eyes roamed through all the items in the store.

A notebook hanging on a wall got my attention. I stopped in front of it to get a better lock. It had a large photo of an image of a red wax seal logo that was almost exactly like the one for our ministry. Leaning closer, I saw the capital letter "M" in the middle of the seal. Still staring, I dug into my purse for my phone, and I took a quick snapshot. In that moment, I quivered feeling His love and peace.

What does this mean, Lord?

In a soft gentle voice I heard God say,

"You are mine. My promises are *yes* and *Amen* and they are for you now!"

These signs were significant anchors to strengthen my faith to keep moving forward. They were markers along this journey on what God said He would do. He is the same yesterday, today, and forevermore!

Recalling the great things God has done in our lives, reminds us, He can do it once again. He's our rescuer, lover, deliverer; and what an amazing God He is!

REMEMBERING WHAT GOD HAS DONE
OPENS US FOR CONTINUED MIRACLES IN
OUR LIVES.

He is the God of miracles, not disappointments. We need to keep our focus on Him.

In 1 Kings 18:20-40, there's a show down between Elijah the prophet, and King Ahab at Mt. Carmel. Elijah challenges Ahab atop this mountain and whosoever god showed up, will rule.

Jezabel, King Ahab's wife had a strong influence and convinced 850 false prophets to be under her. She had just massacred hundreds of true prophets, and Elijah, representing a true prophet, was going to win the hearts of the people back toward God through this stand down, with the intention of annihilating her false prophets. Jezabel, on the other hand represented idolatry and she'd convinced others into idol (Baal) worship. If you read the story in it's entirety, (1 Kings 16 - 2 Kings 6), you will see how profound this story ends. This story makes a point, that God will show up for those that belong to Him, with power to destroy the work of the enemy. We must believe with our faith and stand down the enemy, not allowing him to intimidate us to back down when God has already promised.

Elijah had set 12 stones of remembrance around his altar with confidence that God would come through on that altar, with real fire and power when Elijah called down His God. When He's shown up already 12 times then you know he's not going to let you down in that particular moment.

Almighty God showed up just like He promised for his people and rendered Ahab's god and eight hundred and fifty of Jezabel's false prophets dead on Mt. Carmel.

I was reminded of many miracles God had done for me over the years. God brought back specific memories. I took every stone of remembrance, of what God had done in my life, gathered them together, and laid them before the Throne of God in the Heavens. We talked about each one, and I encouraged myself in the Lord during that season. Just like He did for Elijah, all He'd done in the past for me was miraculous too, and He wasn't about to leave me hanging now.

I recalled how He healed me of cancer in 2005. It was an eight-inch mass tumor on the right side of my pelvis was found in the ER. I was told I needed to have an emergency surgery, and I declined it, went home and had some other doctors take a look at it. Three doctors confirmed it was cancer.

A woman at the church we attended prayed for me. She had a strong gift of healing and she insisted on praying for me several times. One of those times, she came to me at church because she had a dream about me.

Wow, God, you put me on the heart of a woman I barely know?

I felt loved by God in an unusual way in that moment. She laid her hands on me and declared Mark 11:20 where it says, "Now in the morning, as they passed by, they saw the fig tree dried up from the roots." She continued to pray and take authority over the tumor commanding it to wither up and die.

I had the surgery, and the surgeon came out of the operating room declaring to my husband in the waiting room what she had prayed. The surgeon was perplexed and with astonishment, said to my husband,

"It was as if it severed from the root lost its blood supply and withered up and died!"

He didn't call it cancer anymore. When they sent it to pathology, it came back there was NO trace of cancer in the tumor. So many times God shows me His love and kindness. I'm undone and enamored by such grace He gives me in some of the darkest situations, I've found myself in. This pronounces the incredible privilege we've been given to belong to Jesus.

We are made with a DNA to remember the goodness of God. The enemy flings negative memories from our past to keep us locked up and ineffective to the things of His Kingdom. But we were created to remember all the good things He's done. When we actually meditate on His good works and all of the goodness of our Heavenly Father, it creates an atmosphere of more goodness to continue in our lives.

He had healed me of an eight-inch mass tumor that three doctors declared was cancer in 2005, and He healed me of panic attacks, insomnia, depression and anxiety in 1996.

• • •

I remember another profound time when God assured me He would do the impossible and sent angles to help me.

What an amazing miracle when two angels miraculously recovered my lost key. Let me share....

Still groggy around 7 a.m., I took my dog, Savannah, out for an early morning run around Miramar Lake. It's our usual routine: I got Savannah out of the car, removed my key from the key chain, locked the doors, and shoved some poop bags and key into the right pocket of my hoodie. I turned on my mp3, and we were off for a five-mile run.

Savannah loved people and liked to slow down and stare at every person that goes by hoping someone will stop to pet her. If that weren't enough, she'll stop to sniff the variety of bushes and flowers along this colorful trail. I'd nudge her along for the first mile until she'd focus and realize this was not a sniffing trip.

I finally coaxed her into a good pace, when I looked up and saw a couple coming from the opposite direction. They talked and smiled, taking extra notice of Savannah as they walked by us. I didn't think anything of this until later.

When we finished the run, I was nearing my car, and dug into my pocket for my car key and it wasn't there! Frantic, I searched through all my pockets. I had always been conscientious of the loose key when I run, and had never lost it in the eight years of running with Savannah. Usually, I'd put the key in a deep pocket or one with a zipper, but not on this particular morning.

It must have fallen out when I pulled the poop bags to collect Savannah's first "morning offerings."

Now what am I suppose to do? I don't have a cell phone or an extra key.

My key was gone. Shaking with panic, I backtracked my earlier steps. Fighting the accusing thoughts,

"How could you be so careless? You never put your key in that pocket. Why today? You should have been paying attention."

My eyes darted, searching the grounds, as I pleaded with the Lord, "Please send me an angel to help!"

Even though the onslaught of negative thoughts kept attacking. "What am I going to do? I don't want to call my husband. He'd come to my rescue but boy would he be mad to have to leave work right now in the middle of a hectic schedule."

While looking around for someone to come to my aid, I recognized my attitude.

I had agreed with every berating thought. The Holy Spirit got a hold of me. *"Forgive yourself for losing it and don't agree with that fear right now!"*

I pulled myself together, as I continued pacing the grounds for the missing key. Muttering under my breath, "I forgive myself...I forgive myself...I forgive myself."

"...And fear go right now. I ask you Lord to forgive me for listening to these accusations. I repent and in the name of Jesus, I command this fear to go!"

I spotted some older gentlemen who are "regulars" when I run. *I think they look kind enough to help me in my predicament.*

I caught one's attention and boldly announced, "I lost my car key!"

His eyes grew wide. Then, both men came closer asking me a flurry of questions. One man offered his cell phone. Then he mentioned he would leave me in the care of his friend as he was going to go for a bike ride. His unnamed friend began looking around my car and in the nearby bushes.

As I scoured the grounds, I repeated, "Holy Spirit lead me to this key."

Dirt and bark were everywhere amongst sleeping ducks in this park area. How could this key ever be found? It could be anywhere. Not as much as a clink did I hear when it fell.

As I continued to pace back and forth, indignation fueled me to not give up. Satan was not going to win. I was not going to think about how to solve this problem in a natural way. Instead, I kept saying to myself, "Stay focused Maria... Stay focused on Jesus."

In that moment, overwhelming faith rose up inside me as I prayed, "Father your Word says, Ask for anything in Your Name and you will do it. I am asking for a miracle. I need a miracle right now, Father!"

Within less than two minutes, I walked, head down and eyes riveted to the pavement, when I heard a woman ask, "What are you looking for?"

"This woman lost her car key," the man helping me responded.

"Oh, I found your key," she said.

I jerked my head up and looked in their direction. To my surprise, there stood the couple I saw smiling at Savannah. *How could they be here?* They were walking in opposite direction of us. It makes no sense. There's no way they could be here in that amount of time.

I ran to this woman and embraced her. Emotion overtook me and I broke into tears. She warmly consoled me saying, "It's okay. I put your key on this kiosk over here."

"Thank you so much." I blubbered with tears.

She rested her hand on my shoulder, "I always find keys."

This couple kindly guided me to the key sitting safely on the lip of a large kiosk. She placed the key in my hand.

I looked up at heaven and shouted, "Thank you Jesus!" I took the key, lifting it up in the air and directly looked into her eyes saying, "This is a miracle."

They never flinched at any of my comments about Jesus or miracles. Their countenance was strangely gentle and didn't seem to react to my comments.

"Were they angels?" I believe they were.

I got into my car, still overtaken by emotion, I started the ignition and a song started playing from the CD in the car stereo. It was about God's love. Struck by his care for me, I bent over weeping, with my hands in my face, in utter awe of His goodness.

Inundated by the love of my Father, I then heard, "I did this for you. You could not have done this for yourself. I fixed this for YOU. I did this because I want you to know how much I love you."

The next day, I planned to minister at an Aglow meeting in the morning. This miracle caused my faith to soar to another level. At the end of that meeting many were healed and one woman's tumor dissolved.

Remembering His goodness in times of trial stirs up our faith to keep our relationship with God in tact. It enables us to connect at a deeper level with Him through recalling His goodness in every situation.

Instead of focusing on the problem, we can fix our eyes on the solution. Being solution focused instead of problem focused, brings the answers we need.

By meditating on God's goodness, and focusing our attention on remembering all that He's done we project faith into the situation instead of fear. Which eventually attracts His goodness for a better outcome. It stirs up the awe of God and a focal point of praise.

Psalm 78 shows us to focus on the good works, because of all He's done.

Psalm 78:4-7, 12

4 "We will not hide *them* from their children,

Telling to the generation to come the praises of the LORD,

And His strength and His wonderful works that He

has done.

5 For He established a testimony in Jacob,

And appointed a law in Israel,

Which He commanded our fathers,

That they should make them known to their children;

6 That the generation to come might know *them*,

The children *who* would be born,

That they may arise and declare *them* to their children,

7 That they may set their hope in God,

And not forget the works of God,

But keep His commandments,"

And then it says this in verse

12 "Marvelous things He did in the sight of their fathers,

In the land of Egypt, *in* the field of Zoan."

When we get healed and touched by God in a powerful way, we experience the awe of His goodness. When we praise Him we are simply boasting of the nature of God and His miraculous works.

Once you have an encounter with God how do you sustain the awe?

When we lose the awe of God we'll get stagnant and become prey to the enemy weakening us. Then a critical spirit comes through our erroneous opinions.

Also, disappointments can cause us to lose our focus off of Jesus and onto those negative things exalting themselves above God. Then we lose the awe and wonder of who God is.

I chose to praise God in the midst of those disappointments. In that place of worship and rest, He lifted the burden of it, and eased the pain as the process continued. This is a key to not only sustain your ground but to live a lifestyle of living higher in His rest.

When we lose the awe and wonder of God, we forget what God has done. Our relationship with Him is sustained by continual praising of all He's done in our lives. We rest in what He's already done knowing He will bring us through the battle unscathed.

We can't allow ourselves to forget what God's done in the past or the enemy will then introduce lies and offenses that slowly steal the life out of us.

I look for places where God is working or doing miracles to keep me aware of His splendor, always keeping my attention on how glorious He really is.

These "power encounters" change everything. In a moment of experiencing His mighty love, our perspective can shift and we now see only His goodness and love instead of the hurt, conflict, or disappointment.

God is rooting for us. He's always looking out for our best interests. What good dad doesn't want to give good gifts to those that belong to Him? As our Heavenly Father, He also wants an amazing relationship filled with awe and wonder.

When we keep our gaze upon our Heavenly Father, we have an opportunity to leave a legacy of God's goodness to the next generation. The God's awe and wonder will torch the appetite of an entire nation; that's exactly what happened to Israel.

Joshua 24:31 says, "Israel served the LORD all the days of Joshua, and all the days of the elders who outlived Joshua, who had known all the works of the LORD which He had done for Israel."

But then they sinned and didn't believe His works. In that time, they tempted God and limited Him. They put a cap on what God could do. They lost sight of who He was and what He meant by the decree that "nothing is impossible with God".

They forgot their won history. They lost sight of what God had done for them and all the wonderful miracles time and time again, where He delivered them from harms way so many times.

Do you recall the good things God has done in your past when the pressure starts to get heavy? When bad circumstances arise the best way to strengthen yourself is meditate on His goodness. Another way, is remembering all He's done for you.

DO YOU REMEMBER ALL THE MIRACLES HE'S DONE IN YOUR LIFE?

Don't forget them. One way is to write them down. When you're in a bind or something hard has hit you; go back to that list and recall those good things and strike the enemy with those stones of remembrance. He will cause the enemy to flee and you now are positioning yourself to receive more of God's grace, peace, and love.

What moved them into a place where they had forgotten what God could do? They forgot their own personal history. When we forget or lose track of what is on God's heart, we forget where we have come from!

THE GREATEST MIRACLE IS OUR OWN CONVERSION.

A spiritual discipline and a way to activate your ability to hear and remember better is to meditate on the good works of God. It keeps you saying "yes" and hearing and seeing God deeper.

The moment you stop dreaming, you start dying. Living to take continual risks will push us to believe for "the more" of God and will stir our hunger, that will never to fade away again.

When we engage with God like this, we keep an attitude that enables us to leave a legacy of God's goodness to the next generation.

Heavenly Perspective

THE LAW AND THE PROPHETS WERE UNTIL JOHN.
SINCE THAT TIME THE KINGDOM OF GOD HAS BEEN
PREACHED, AND EVERYONE IS PRESSING INTO IT.

LUKE 16:16

GOD HAS THE LAST say in everything. Wait it out. Stand on the promises of God, recall the goodness of what He's done, and before you know it He's done what He always said He'd do. This is foundational for you to see a miracle come to pass in the midst of any fire storm.

While you're pressing into God, seeking His face and resting in Him, He does things you'd probably never anticipate.

FAITH IS A SUBSTANCE; IT'S THE VEHICLE THAT BRINGS YOUR MIRACLE

As we obey His voice, we persevere through all the bad reports, cynics, and negative rhetoric interrupting our peace.

A person who gets a diagnosis like cancer is all of sudden surrounded by experts with advice on how to get better. Eat right! Take medicine! Do this! Do that! It's annoying, and maddening, to listen to all the opinions. At some point early on, I made a decision to not talk about the cancer. I didn't tell my family I had cancer. I didn't tell most of the people around me. I definitely wasn't going to make any more room to be caught in a tailspin of negative chatter over this. Although, we came in contact with a lot of people because of our ministry, only a few close friends knew. Over the months, several more knew but honored my request to keep it on the down low. A few couldn't do that. However, I know that's normal, I suppose, when someone you care about is sick. They feel the person's pain. I think most people are well intentional.

Some, weren't as nice by the callous words they blurted. I tried not to be offended by some people's reactions, because they were taken by my choices to not tell any of them until after the fact.

I needed to do what's best for myself in the healing process. I chose not to discuss it. These decisions are very personal especially when your life is threatened. If I did talk about it, I would get agitated and fearful. Explaining the details over and over would put me on an emotional roller coaster with an high-octane ping of adrenaline flashing through my being. Then, there was the constant retelling of details about the cancer to every doctor, nurse, x-ray tech I came in contact with. It was Exhausting!

Meanwhile, I spent most of my time focused on resting in His love and peace. This was my "happy" place. For the most part, I was able to avoid a lot of negative rhetoric and stay close to God. I only talked with those people who prayed and encouraged me concerning the miracle that was coming. I could see and hear God better when I was dialed back to listen more intently. After all, His voice is often quiet and still.

When we continually say "Yes" to God even in the midst of the worst situations, His grace enables us to: stand up, stay strong, and shine for Him right in the midst of the chaos. In the weakest moments of our lives He shines the brightest.

During this season of standing and waiting on Him, I was asked to speak on healing to at a local church discipleship school in San Diego.

How am I going to preach on healing when I am sick?

God qualifies us. We're qualified to be partakers of the inheritance in the saints. He gave us this amazing sonship through the Father's love. We belong to Him. As His sons and daughters, we've been given an inheritance that qualifies us to do the "stuff". In other words, regardless of what we are dealing with during our process, God still uses us to demonstrate His power and authority to destroy the works of the devil. If we continue to strive to live a righteous life, somehow His grace covers us, and He shines through us.

That's exactly what happened in that meeting that night I taught on healing.

I recall stepping up to the platform and sensing the overwhelming presence and love of God. The audience was so receptive, and as I taught on healing many were touched by God's love and power and received healing. I recall one guy, who texted someone in the Philippines while I was calling out words of knowledge. That guy in the Philippines received healing through a text.

At the end of the meeting, I invited anyone who wanted to have an anointing to heal others and to be filled with a baptism of the Holy Spirit to come forward. Two hundred hungry people of all ages lined up. Pressed against the walls, crammed tightly around the perimeter of the room, expectation arose, to encounter God. Sandwiched in between two male ministry leaders, like my body guards they moved along the wall with me praying for each person, as I gently placed my fingers in their open hands. They'd get blasted by the power of God and either be filled with joy laughing, crying or on the ground encountering the power of God. At one point, I directed the two men with me to start laying hands on the people. The anointing of God only increased and they saw many blasted by God through them. Not only were any were many being touched powerfully by God, but these two leaders got ignited knowing God could use them.

That powerful night with the Holy Spirit was spectacular. It was a life-changing day for many of those students. The most eye-opening revelation that day for me was to realize even when we're in the midst of our own struggles, we should never stop, or minimize our effectiveness for God and the purposes He's called us to. If we are sick, we can still pray for the sick to be healed. When God asks you to do something, He's equipped you to do it and do it powerfully!

I didn't stop ministering after the diagnosis. We carried on with our weekly Red Seal meetings. Rick and I usually traded off teaching each week.

The week I was diagnosed, I took time to regroup from the shock of the news. As I felt I was supposed to step back and spending more time with God, one of our friends, Bill Dew, who's traveled the world and seen many thousands healed by the power of God, encouraged me that day. He said,

"Go after breast cancer. It's pay back Maria."

Oh really?

It was in that moment it dawned on me to push through the enemy's tactic to get me to shut down!

That following week I spoke at our Tuesday night meeting. Focusing on the issues surrounding rejection, I invited people to get free from any fear of rejection or anger from being rejected by others. After the teaching we did an alter call for healing as we do each week. What took place blew me away. My prayer line formed in front of me as they usually do each week, but this week four women with breast cancer came forward for prayer!

I recall, one woman in particular, Beatriz, who continued to come to the meetings each week. She came to my line for about six weeks. She'd been diagnosed with stage-three breast cancer, on the right side, a tumor the size of a lemon. One week, the Holy Spirit prompted me to ask Beatriz,

"Would you be open to some personal ministry time?"

"Yes, of course." She replied.

That night, I took her into a side room off the sanctuary. Bringing an assistant, we went to work and prayed with her for over an hour.

We uncovered some roots and doors open to the enemy from her troubled past. At three years old she was sexually violated and again at seven years old. Both incidents brought deeply rooted pain from the trauma that was never dealt with.

Beatriz gave us permission to walk her through some prayers for forgiveness. That night her countenance changed drastically.

She came back to Red Seal the following week looking amazing. I sensed God had done something spectacular. The next week she ran to me,

"My tumor is not a lemon size anymore, it's now the size of an almond!"

"Really, that's amazing Beatriz ." I responded.

"Do you want to see?" She asked.

I was taken aback she'd say that but I sensed with her excitement and surprise she wanted me to know that the prayers worked!

"Okay."

She grabbed my hand and placed it where the tumor was.

"I can't even feel it."

"I know it's there, but it shrunk Maria!"

Beatriz called me several days later from the ICU. She was admitted, because she continued doing chemo, even though the tumor was gone. I prayed with her over the phone and I used my words in that prayer to declare all toxicity be removed her body. I declared she be released from the hospital within 24 hours.

She notified me that she was indeed released and completely better the next day. Not only were the doctors flabbergasted she got better so fast, but also how the tumor at this point was microscopic and almost invisible.

Her story continued as she underwent a lumpectomy and there was nothing there and no cancer visible in the area or anywhere in her body!

Several other women were healed that month of breast cancer and all of these women needed to deal with unforgiveness issues. In the ministry we learned that unforgiveness is the number one block to healing.

When we look at ourselves as a body, soul, and spirit, then we are more open to view ourselves from a perspective that relies on seeing our healing, from a standpoint that involves looking at all three aspects. We don't just treat one without treating all other parts.

1 Thessalonians 5:23 says, "Now may the God of peace Himself sanctify you completely; and may your *whole spirit, soul, and body* be preserved blameless at the coming of our Lord Jesus Christ."

In other words, changing your diet is good, but if you never deal with the root issues of the heart, you may not get healed. Trying to cure cancer just through diet, and with only that perspective, is not going to necessarily defeat it. Just the same, dealing with unforgiveness or sin issues and not changing your diet to eliminate sugar and bad fats, may not bring about health improvements either.

We must recognize we are three in one. We are a body; take a look at our vessel and the house we live in. I call it our mobile home. Not every mobile home looks alike. We come in all shapes and sizes. Some are highly decorated and some are simple. We are the temple of God. We can choose to position ourselves for the healing by caring for ourselves. By making the necessary changes to achieve a healthy lifestyle we will enjoy a life that is in the physical realm, as well as the spiritual and emotional dimensions.

When we overcome in an area in our lives we have authority in that place. God's given us the authority, because of our faith and because we defeated that area.

God was giving me an anointing to heal breast cancer even though I wasn't yet healed of the cancer.

That year we saw several others healed of cancer. I recall one woman who had a brain tumor, and she came forward and fell under the power of God. The following year she revisited Red Seal and stood up and shared how that night when she fell over she felt heat, and an overwhelming peace of God. When she went back to her doctor to get another scan, no tumor was visible.

A Chinese woman came to one of our meetings and a softball size tumor was on her liver. We prayed for her and she forgave a man who'd sexually violated her at a young age. We then prayed over the tumor, it literally disappeared! My hand dropped and my assistant and myself looked at each other in shock! I'd like to say I had a lot of faith in that moment; but I was surprised. I hadn't seen God do that before. It's amazing to experience God's power in these moments. We celebrated the goodness of God right there.

Another time we were at a large church meeting in San Diego where Randy Clark had been asked to minister. My husband and I were part of his ministry team. I remember a friend from Mexico brought a pastor from Tijuana to me for prayer. This woman pastor had three walnut size tumors under her jaw area. When I prayed and I felt fire come from my hands. As I commanded the tumor to go I swished my hand briskly across the area and felt the tumors completely dissolve from under my hand. We jumped up and down causing a ruckus in that church and many more lined up around us for prayer. The testimony of Jesus is the spirit of prophesy. (Revelation 19: 22)

When we share the goodness of God we are positioning ourselves to receive another miracle. You may be reading this and need a miracle; receive the blessing of these miracles and take it for yourself.

Somehow, when some people know you are sick, they want to help by sharing their worst horror stories and the gruesome details of when they were sick too! This is not something anyone wants to hear when trying to stir up faith for God to move in the midst of a battle. It amazed me how some people are so oblivious and insensitive in times in our worst times! Perhaps, you know people like this too? Don't allow yourself to be offended. You can move forward and steer your focus back on what's important and that's God's Truth and love.

Cancer is from the devil! Bottom line. There's no argument. God didn't cause it, nor does he use it to teach us a lesson! God doesn't need to attack you to correct you either. Satan has been clever to use anything to trick us to blame God for bad things happening in our lives. He wants to destroy us. God created us in His image. The devil's just jealous of us. Why? Because Satan ever since that day when Lucifer challenged God (Isaiah 14), he was kicked out of Heaven. Did you know that Lucifer was one of God's adored and one of His high ranking angelic beings as the most ultimate worshiper? He covered the throne of God and led worship! He was evicted from Heaven. His pride cost him. He told God he was going to be God. Take the Creator's position? He's going to tell God how it works? In that moment of pride he lost it all! Kicked out of Heaven for good.

Lucifer, who is now Satan, comes against God's chosen beloved creations to convince us with pride that God is trying to withhold something good from us. God is good and Satan isn't. This spiritual battle we are in; is for us to continually choose the goodness of God. Satan knows it.

Satan is an equal opportunity oppressor. God's love is endless and His motivation is for us to always grasp the height, depth and width of His love. God is good. We were created to encounter God and live in an experience of His love our entire lives.

I don't know about you, but when God speaks I want to listen. His voice definitely determines my direction. I will choose daily to keep autocorrecting my thoughts and actions to match those of my Father's in Heaven.

A specific word from the Lord catapults you forward to sustain you in the battle. He always confirms what he's doing in times of trial.

His Word establishes a foundation, in us so we won't shatter under the pressure of difficulties. I stayed focused on Mark 9:23 through most of this season.

Mark 9:23 says, "If you believe, all things are possible to those that believe."

I determined in my heart, that my decisions would be to be dictated by Him and not influenced by any outside sources. It was difficult to wade through the sludge, but when God gives you a Word, you can bank on His promise.

Pressing into God, I kept asking God for signs and confirmations about the healing from cancer.

I want to hear from a prophet.

Prompted by the Holy Spirit in that moment, I pursued a life coaching session with Doug Addison, by contacting his ministry. I called in on my scheduled date in September to receive a thirty-minute personal coaching session.

Doug got on the line and there were two of us callers on the same line!

What's happening here?

He sorted it out and allowed me to get the call! Thank you God for favor.

During the first five minutes, Doug released a prophetic word.

In that word he mentions,

"... You are experiencing a lot of warfare and a spirit of confusion is attacking you. I know that because of the way we got on your call. I've never experienced two people on the call at the same time and that's confusion."

He prayed and took authority over it and continued on with my word.

He said,

"You will receive a healing in your body for something. You also have a business anointing that comes from your mother's side of the family..."

After he gave the word he shared how he had recently received healing and just gotten back into the country. It was an amazing time of encouragement and confirmation from Doug. The word solidified what God had been showing me in the previous few months.

Words like this give us a Heavenly perspective and they change our lens to see through God's eyes. The world's view is that of a foreigner. People don't know what you are called to do, and they won't be there to help you fulfill it.

These words from the Holy Spirit bring stability in the storm. Grounding ourselves in His promises, establish and anchor our faith to be unshaken.

Through the waiting, we stand on His Words specifically to keep our faith cheering for the victory.

Every prophetic word is a snapshot of God's intent for your future. Our God in His greatness sets a piece of your future in front of you into the present through that word. Doesn't it motivate you to move forward? The prophetic it's designed to encourage you to have hope and push forward. It empowers us to press through the resistance and step into the future that God is inviting us into.

Promises keep you connected to that divine destiny in God and prevent you from settling for anything less than what He's called for you.

A word from God keeps us mindful of a constant purpose and great destiny awaiting us. It's essential if we are to move forward in our growth as mature believers. It constantly reminds us of who God is and what He is capable of doing in and through us.

Israel didn't stay mindful of her destiny, and as a result her collapse was incredibly destructive. The people lost sight of their destiny. The opposite is also true. As you consider your destiny in God, as revealed by His promise, it moves you forward and onward to fulfill your potential and walk out your purpose.

If you are a believer, then you know that you've inherited every one of God's promises.

CAN YOU RECALL WORDS SPOKEN OVER YOU?

How about the prophetic words that have not come to pass yet? I mean ones that are legit? Ones you know where confirmed and you're pressing into God for them to come to pass?

I learned from Bill Johnson, to pray over our prophetic words frequently and come into agreement with them until they manifest in your life. That revelation helped me get a better perspective while I waited on the promise of my healing from the cancer.

We are called to cultivate faith and pray into the prophetic words and not just let them sit. We may forget them if we have an "oh, that was nice" attitude about those words. Then they just fall to the wayside and become dead.

We must receive well the promises and words spoken over us. Prophetic words don't always just come to pass on their own. We must cultivate faith by declaring them and believing in the His promise of that sure word.

His Word is unchanging.

Hebrews 10:38 says, "He who promised is faithful."

It's one thing to believe that God is faithful and it is another thing to actually have a revelation of His faithfulness in action.

FAITH IS TRUST IN ACTION.

When you receive a prophetic word, you believe it. When you trust what God has said, you confidently move toward it.

Hebrews 11:8 says, "By faith Abraham obeyed when he was called to go out to the place which he would receive as an inheritance. And he went out, not knowing where he was going."

Mary heard that word from the angel and she said as a response in Luke 1:38, "Let it be to me according to your word. And also we see it in." Then, Luke 1:37 says, "For with God nothing will be impossible."

No freshly spoken Word from God will ever come to you that does not contain the ability to be performed.

God sent His Word and it's able to perform what it says.

The power of those promises of God increases our understanding of why we can trust the faithfulness of the One who promises. God gives us the promises to draw us and invite us into our destiny.

CHAPTER 6

Healing Breakthrough

BEHOLD, I WILL BRING IT HEALTH AND HEALING;
I WILL HEAL THEM AND REVEAL TO THEM THE
ABUNDANCE OF PEACE AND TRUTH.

JEREMIAH 33:6

FIVE MONTHS HAD PASSED since the initial diagnosis of breast cancer. Scan after scan was becoming comical. I was scheduled for yet another scan at another medical facility. This was going to be my eighth scan. I diligently kept all these appointments to obtain an accurate assessment of my situation.

Under my surgeon's recommendation we went to his facility for this new ultrasound. All the other scans came from another facility and this surgeon wanted one of his doctors at this particular facility to confirm the findings.

I had already been to this office once before, but due to insurance issues I couldn't get the scan last time. It was like running around in circles. I knew they wanted to be extremely sure of their findings before doing the surgery and I wasn't too keen on being rushed in to being cut open. The wait between scans for approvals from my insurance company, gave me more time to pray.

With a 7:00 a.m. appointment, I was the first one in. A cheerful woman who was the X ray technician and her assistant-in-training greeted me, and instructed me to change into a white sterile gown. Her assistant's back was to me, making small talk as I changed quickly. I sat on the bed next to the computer screen. I shared my faith as she swiveled her chair around staring into the screen, and she asked me a slew of pertinent questions. I shared how I was healed of a cancer tumor on 2005.

Disinterested she continued in a matter-of-fact manner toward me, and stayed with her agenda doing the ultrasound.

I hope this won't take long.

When, the main technician, Melissa, came into the room, she said,

"I don't seem to have all your previous scans," as she looked intently into the computer screen.

"What are we scanning here today?"

"I have incito carcinoma on the left side, right here," I said as I pointed to the area.

Patiently, I laid down on the bed, as the ultrasound got under way. I shared with Melissa, how I was healed of an eight-inch mass tumor in 2005, when she asked me my previous medical history. I always like to see the reaction of unbelief on the medical professionals faces when I share what happened.

As she rolled the ultra sound wand around the right breast area, the warm gel glided easily, and she continued to make more conversation. Soon she became more at ease and shared,

" I had breast cancer, too, three years ago. It was on the left side and, was about a three inch mass. I went through chemo and radiation but I just found out last week the cancer came back there again!"

"Oh my! I'm sorry to hear that." I responded.

All of sudden, in the midst of our conversation, a perplexed look crossed her face, as she was glanced at her other computer screen. Worry became more apparent, and then, she said,

"I don't seem to have any of your scans from any of the other places. It may take a while to get these. But I can't proceed with this until we have these all in my hands first."

Her tone changed. "Wait here." She retained her kind demeanor, but now upset, she abruptly ran out of the room.

She came back to the room about 30 minutes later and stood next to me. Peering directly into my eyes, as I lay on the bed, she said,

"You have cancer on the right side too!"

"No I don't." I replied boldly.

"Yes, you do."

In a sort of sarcastic manner, I laughed. Still keeping my composure I remarked,

"I do not have cancer on the right side. You need to go back and check that again."

A look of, "maybe I should listen to her" emerged on her face. Pausing and not saying anything, she put her hand on my shoulder,

"I'll be right back."

What the heck is going on around here? Cancer on the right side too, Lord? This is going from bad to worse.

I'd been there for over an hour and still hadn't gotten the scan.

Rick was outside in the waiting room. He often liked to take me to all my appointments as a support to me.

Rick is wondering what happened to me!

By this time, the technician came back into the room and asked me to get up and wait in another waiting room until they could sort it all out.

I was escorted to a modern and nicely decorated waiting room with TV screens and books. Anything I needed to occupy one's mind. I chose to pray.

Holy Spirit I need your help. How do I pray?

I prayed in tongues, waited, and listened. About 20 minutes later, I heard a voice say within me,

"I want you to pray for the woman technician, Melissa."

"I don't want to Lord. This is about me right now." I responded with self- pity.

I recognized by my reaction to God's invitation, I was battling the fear of what was happening. There was a long silence. Then, I heard,

"Take authority over the confusion."

I began to pray,

"I command all confusion to leave now in Jesus name. God, break off anything the enemy is trying to do to get things off course."

As soon as I prayed, less that thirty seconds went by, and the technician bolted through the door with a white paper in her hand and exclaimed,

"Okay, at 7:05 it reads in the biopsy report you had cancer on the right side, but at 7:11 it says no cancer there!"

Oh thank Heaven, for 7-11.

She brought me back into the room and as we were walking to the room God reminded me of what He'd asked me to do while praying.

We finished the ultra sound and she kept saying,

"Well, I don't see anything else that the MRI is showing. I am not going to try to find something that isn't there."

Soon after she was done, a doctor came in to look over the scans and released me to go.

I'd been sharing my faith the entire time Melissa was doing the ultrasound. We had plenty of time together. By now, almost two and half-hours went by, and she was receptive to me sharing all my testimonies about what God had done in my life. I sensed her openness.

The other gal, the assistant, silently observed and showed me early on her disinterest in God. However, Melissa seemed open to listening. She'd endured a battle and there was tenderness toward those who were going through the same battle as her. She was gentle, compassionate and certainly hated cancer too.

By now the doctor had left the room and it was only Melissa and the assistant in the room.

"Okay, looks like this party is over Maria!"

I got up off the bed and asked,

"Melissa, may I pray for you?"

Her eyes lit up and said,

"Yes, thank you!"

"Can I put my hand on you?"

"Sure." She answered.

I gently placed my hand on her shoulder and prayed,

"God, take this cancer now from Melissa's body. I command all cancer cells to go and bring every cell into order. I release healing into her body now. I declare no cancer and when she goes back to the doctor this cancer will be gone in Jesus name."

After I was done praying, Melissa embraced me tightly. She wouldn't let me go. We embraced at what seemed minutes. Afterward, she opened the door and escorted me out.

I believe in that moment, she felt loved. She felt someone understood, but more importantly she heard my faith that impossible things are possible.

The next morning, I stumbled into the kitchen at six am. Rick was already up reading the daily newspaper. He's one of those that still liked to read the San Diego Union Tribune early in the morning with a hot cup of freshly brewed coffee.

He lifted his eyes from reading and insisted I listen to an article he was reading. Listen to this, Maria, "Many women in San Diego are being diagnosed with incito carcinoma and Canadian researchers have discovered that after 10 years of thorough scientific results, many, if not all, of these women never see the calcifications or cell clusters grow into tumors. These cells stay that way and don't change!"

I stood leaning against the kitchen counter dumbfounded by such news.

I sensed Gods presence and His affirming me once again fending off any doubt I may have had in this process. I felt His embracing His love; I knew He wasn't going to let anything happen to me in this process. Encouragement was reinforced once again by what we read in this article.

• • •

We had scheduled a mission trip with Global Awakening, and Randy Clark, the leader of this ministry who is a known healing minister, yearly, takes teams to Brazil.

The teams are equipped, and released to minister alongside Randy Clark where they experience the power of God and see thousands healed of many sickness and diseases.

My husband, Rick had gone the year before and was enamored by the power of God and the incredible testimonies of many people being healed while he was doing ministry there. The team has translators and they work with people

On Rick's trip, the team ministered in several Brazilian churches and over 400 people were healed from many physical ailments.

Rick shared with me one of the highlights of his trip. On the first night, one miracle in particular literally challenged his faith to believe bigger for miracles.

He was ministering with the team, when he hears in the distance, someone in another line, let out a chilling scream.

Rick sensed something amazing was happening and pushed his way through the crowd and ran to see first hand what was happening. Apparently, when she was 8 years old, she was in an accident where she lost her eye.

In the service, one of the team prayed for her and the glass eye popped out. A milky substance began to recreate. Rick was able to watch this entire process. After the 3rd day of being there, they brought this woman up on stage to testify of the healing and revealed the miracle of her perfect new eye!!

Rick was so excited by all he experienced he insisted I go back with him. We had set up this trip to Sao Paulo, Brazil a year in advance, before I was diagnosed with the cancer. We told the oncologist about the trip, he approved our travels, and instructed when we returned from Brazil he would do the surgery.

We left for a two-week trip at the end of September. It was everything I imagined and more. Hundreds of people touched by God in many different Brazilian churches, large and small.

Blaine Cooke was on this trip and he was one of the most instrumental people in my life. He traveled with John Wimber during the Jesus movement. He ignites many people into the healing ministry and was now traveling with Randy on these trips releasing people into their destiny to move in power.

When these ministering teams leave these cities, and people who get radically touched by God usually start ministries of their own, and move in the same anointing as these ministers.

Blaine prayed for me over 20 years ago in a small white church called Coast Vineyard in La Jolla, a coastal city in San Diego.

I clearly recall that day as if it were yesterday. One morning, my friend, Stan took me to a healing meeting in an old, quaint, small white church. That hot summer morning the service was packed with a few hundred people crammed into this old church. Lines and lines of people formed at the altar, waiting for Blaine to pray for them. I never made it into one of those lines. Instead, some elders in the church prayed for us. It all seemed good to me and we left. As we were walking on the sidewalk to the car, my friend stopped me and said,

"We need to go back! I want my friend, Blaine, to pray for you."

We turned around, reentered the church, where the second service was starting. We encountered Blaine praying for the last person in the line, and he agreed to pray for me when a woman from the church insisted we go back into another room. It all happened so fast, I didn't really have time to analyze it.

She escorted us to a broom closet. I'm surrounded by shelves and shelves of cleaning products, like Mr. Clean, bleach and disinfectants, all lined up next to mops, brooms and sponges.

Blaine asked me to look at him. As I stood and looked into his piercing blue eyes, my knees got weak, and all of a sudden I fell to the ground. Trembling and light headed, I allowed Stan to lead me to a small shallow stool where I sat for the next 45 minutes. As he prayed for me, I trembled and shook violently inside. I felt intense pressure, and then it would lift, and then in came incredible, peace. God overtook me with His love and power like I'd never felt before.

How many know that when you have one encounter with God you are never the same?

That day changed the rest of my life forever. I was never the same. I was healed of anxiety, panic attacks, depression and insomnia. I encountered the most incredible peace I'd ever felt and it never left! I experienced the true living God with such fierce love and peace, the only way I can describe it was like liquid love pulsing through my entire being.

I found it fitting I'd experience God this way in a broom closet. Everything unclean left me. God cleaned up. I felt so clean and pure. So full of peace and love that no matter what was happening around me at the time, I felt loved and nothing bothered me.

In that time frame, God set up supernatural appointments with people wherever I went. Many people experienced God where they either felt a new direction, fresh peace and refreshment, or encountered God for the first time with salvation.

That experience with God stirred my faith to know and believe God does the miraculous. It was an ongoing need to see more of God. Once you taste and see that the Lord is good, you know there's always more.

Now, over twenty years later, we're on this mission trip and Blaine is on this trip with us! I sensed God was going to do something special on this trip. Too much pointed to the miracle of being healed of cancer.

I recall having a conversation with one of our intercessors, Anita, who has a strong prophetic gifting. When I shared with her I had the cancer, she exclaimed,

"You'll be healed in Brazil!"

I wanted to believe her. I received that word as from God and stood on it as a confirmation to all the other words I'd gotten during this season.

The last night of this two-week trip, we are at a meeting in a church with about a thousand people in attendance. I remember this hot and humid night. It was late, we were tired, and Rick was back at the hotel sick from a bad flu virus.

I was sitting with my friend Steve, who was on our team from Red Seal, and was on this trip. He was sitting on my right side and this other man named Barry, who was sitting on my left side. He was from New York and he'd been healed of PTSD through Michael Hutchings ministry from Global Awakening. God used Barry to get about seventeen other military guys healed from PTSD too. What I liked about Barry was that he seemed solid. Not an overly emotional guy. I admired who he'd become by all he'd overcome in his life, and how God was using him now. I preface this because what was about to happen I would of never expected.

Randy is leading the meeting, and he calls out cancer as a word of knowledge for people to stand up to be healed. All the Brazilians with cancer in the room responded to the invitation, and stood up.

Steve nudges me, leans over, and whispers,

"Stand up."

I turn and look at him, but I didn't respond.

"Stand up. What are you waiting for?" He says it again in a louder voice.

I'm suddenly confronted with my pride.

I don't want all these people to see me.

I don't like to have any attention on me and especially with this. It was in that moment, a sense of shame flooded me, as if something were wrong with me.

I couldn't escape the emotions, but wasn't' going to be ruled by those feelings. Suddenly I stood up. Randy then said,

"Put your hands on the place where the tumor is."

Really? Ok!

I reluctantly, but obediently, placed my hand across my chest around the left breast. Trying to not look to my right where all my friends stood along a wall watching what was happening. I felt the eyes of every person on me. Even though that was irrational, I pushed past what I was thinking and waited for the next prompting. Randy took authority over cancer and released healing over everyone standing. At some point, I sat down, because I didn't actually have a tumor that would be visible if something left.

As I sat down, I felt this sensation in the area like "Icy Hot" or "Ben Gay". They are topical ointments used for athletes with pain in the body. The impression got stronger as this cool and hot sensation pulsated on the left side.

As I sat down, Barry looked as me with his eyes wide in utter bewilderment and said,

"You have cancer?"

I explained briefly my story and then shared how I was feeling this icy hot all over my left side. He then says,

"I smell it!!"

"What?"

"Yeah, I smell icy hot."

Slowly swiveling my body around, I looked to see if anyone behind me had a tube of icy hot in their hand, but there was none in sight.

I figured Barry was solid guy and if he smelt it, perhaps he was receiving a word of knowledge through smell. How could he smell what I was feeling on the inside?

I believe God was giving me a sign. When we returned back to San Diego, I had scheduled a thermogram (a scan done by heat photography). The military use these and they've been found to be highly accurate in most cases. I chose this one because I wanted a non-invasive approach to another scan and believed that God had done something while I was on the trip.

The scan, was easy, and painless. No radiation and no fuss. As I sat with the technician, she brought Rick into the room where the scan was visible on the computer screen. She showed me how to read the scan with different array of colors showing where signs of cancer would be.

She described the yellow, red and blue zones. Then said to both of us,

"There is nothing here that shows cancer."

Overtaken with relief, I was still not sure I understood her correctly because of her nonchalant demeanor.

"So, no cancer?"

"That's right. Your scan is normal, but you'll need to be aware of these areas." She pointed to some areas above the breasts that showed hormonal change.

My hormones certainly had been changing and required me to change my lifestyle and diet. Then, she went over some key changes to make.

We quietly walked out of the office and then I leaped a few times before we made it to the car. As we drove home, overwhelmed by Gods confirming love, we celebrated the victory.

. . .

Now, fast forward to this year, 2017. I met with my primary care doctor and in a routine visit she wanted to revisit my medical history. Squinting into her computer, to examine my chart, she asks,

"How did your surgery go? Did you get chemo? Did you get radiation?"

Stunned, I respond,

"I didn't do any of that. Remember I told you I was healed in Brazil?"

Looking closely at the notes, she states,

"Oh no. We need to get another mammogram."

"No, I don't do those anymore." I commented.

"Why? Well, what happened to the Surgeon...umm what was his name?"

I walked away from it all. I know I was healed and I did a thermogram that showed no cancer. The conversation progressively got more heated. I agreed to do another ultrasound and it was scheduled.

Later that month, I went in for the ultrasound, but that was not good enough for them and I ended up getting the mammogram. I asked God,

"Why do we have to do all this again?"

Well, the medical world that determined I had this cancer needed to be the same ones to say I no longer had it. I knew God wanted to close the door on this ordeal once and for all.

I got the mammogram. A few weeks later I received a letter in the mail stating that the mammogram was normal and to return next year for a routine yearly visit!

I had an appointment already scheduled with my doctor and it was two days later. As I'm waiting in her office, she blew through the door with astonishment and a smile. She went to her computer and admitted she was quite shocked.

"Well I guess you're really happy by these results?' She exclaimed.

"I didn't ask for this scan. You did. I already knew I was good!"

"Yes." She smiled.

"I only did the mammogram to please you, but actually, I am glad because you only made my testimony iron-clad!"

She laughed because of her shock.

I sensed by our conversation her interest to learn more. She seemed inspired, by such miraculous results, and after eight previous scans showing cancer, now, there's no cancer?

She admitted that this report shocked her entire office. This case was now closed. It was contagious, my doctor also felt the joy I experienced and hugged me before I left her office that afternoon.

The medical results only confirmed the breakthrough healing of what God had already done. After eight scans, and one last mammogram, God brought it full circle showing off His glory.

God exceeds our imagination. He does things better and lets us know how great of a God He is.

I gave my life to Jesus over twenty-four years ago on October 4th, 1992! Remember, I'd mentioned I was healed of that eight-inch mass tumor in my pelvis in 2005? Well, the date of that surgery where they declared no cancer was October 4th! The day Randy Clark called out cancer in that big church in Brazil was also October 4th.

All those times where I was healed were consistently and remarkably tagged on that same glorious day, October 4th,

God was saying, "Ten-four. I hear you loud and clear, Maria!"

God then He heals me of breast cancer in October during Breast Cancer Awareness Month! It amazes me how God knows how to get our attention. He has a sense of humor in the midst of what seems like utter chaos.

Psalm 2:4 says, "He sits in the Heavens on His throne and laughs."

What's God laughing at? He's laughing at the schemes of the enemy. He's defeated him and Satan can't do much. Satan is on a budget. He's limited on what He can do. But our Almighty God has unlimited resources. There isn't anything He can't and won't do for those that belong to Him!

I want to join my Heavenly Father in His perspective of things. He has a much higher vantage point. When it gets foggy, I can just laugh, because then I have the right perspective of what's going on instead of doom and gloom.

He loves to prove to us how real His love is and He goes to great lengths to show us that love.

God still does miracles today. He never stopped doing them. He still likes to show off in the midst of what others would say is impossible.

Maybe you have embraced a lifestyle that shuts miracles out?

I'd like to propose to you that this is your time. Turn to God now and believe for your miracle!

I believe God's miracles are on the rise. More people are hungering to know who He is now than every before. Whatever your hunger may be, just know miracles still happen.

And God has one for you today!

Do not remember the former things,
Nor consider the things of old
behold I am doing a new thing.

ISAIAH 43:18

27079595R00052

Made in the USA
Columbia, SC
25 September 2018